0062444

DATE DUE

2010-11 NMI MISSION EDUCATION RESOURCES

✻ ✻ ✻

BOOKS

AFRICAN VOICES
Compiled by Mark and Nancy Pitts

COLD WINDS, WARM HEARTS
The Church of the Nazarene in Bulgaria
by Teanna Sunberg

CONTAGIOUS COMPASSION
The Life and Ministry of Tom Nees
by Neil B. Wiseman

EXTREME ARGENTINA
by Pat Stockett Johnston

FIRST A FLICKER, THEN A BLAZE
Nazarene Missions in India
by Richard Gammill

THE TOWER OF BABEL WAS A BAD IDEA
The Joy and Agony of Second-Language Learning
by Amy Crofford

✻ ✻ ✻

NEW ADULT MISSION EDUCATION CURRICULUM

EXTREME ARGENTINA

PAT STOCKETT JOHNSTON

Nazarene Publishing House
Kansas City, Missouri

Copyright 2010
Nazarene Publishing House

ISBN 978-0-8341-2481-3

Printed in the United States of America

Editor: Aimee Curtis
Cover Design: Doug Bennett
Interior Design: Sharon Page

Unless otherwise indicated, all Scripture quotations are taken from the *Holy Bible, New International Version*® (NIV®). Copyright © 1973, 1978, 1984 by International Bible Society. Used by permission of Zondervan Publishing House. All rights reserved.

ACKNOWLEDGMENTS

I owe two Extreme Nazarene Ministries staff members much thanks for their help in collecting the set of stories in *Extreme Argentina*—Brent Deakins, Extreme Mobilization Officer, and Brian Tibbs, Extreme Director. Venita Needham also shared stories from her daily newsletters written during the Bruno Radi Convention Center project.

I couldn't have written this book if the following hadn't shared their stories straight from their hearts. Thank you.

Judy Davis
Tom Fitzpatrick
Jim Henderson
Neil Horner
Mike Poe
Brad, Tanya, Robby, and Katie Swartzentruber
Judy Turley
Lonna Vopat
Robin Watters

Pat Stockett Johnston
WriterPat@charter.net
www.patstockettjohnston.com

CONTENTS

Foreword		9
1	Surprise Ending	11
2	God Will Take Care of You	15
3	Hope Conquers All	23
4	Discovering God's New Assignment	41
5	All in the Family	47
6	When a Loss Is a Win	53
7	Band-Aids and Motorcycles Save the Day	63
8	Taking Care of Needs	71
9	A Change of Plans	75
Pronunciation Guide		87

Pat Stockett Johnston and her husband, Gordon, served for 34 years as global missionaries for the Church of the Nazarene in Lebanon, Jordan, and Papua New Guinea. They now reside in Temple City, California, where they fulfill their dream of having their own garden by growing chrysanthemums for show.

After graduation from Pasadena Nazarene College (now Point Loma Nazarene University), Pat became a pastor's wife, taught for six years in public schools, and earned a master of arts degree from California State University, Los Angeles. Pat is an ordained minister in the Church of the Nazarene. The Johnstons have four children (Beverly, Keith, Joanne, Craig) and seven grandchildren.

As a freelance writer, Pat's articles have been published in *Holiness Today*, *World Mission Magazine*, and other denominational magazines. She is a regular contributor to the devotional books *Reflecting God* (formerly *Come Ye Apart*) and *Light from the Word*. Pat has written five books for Nazarene Missions International: *Should I Kiss or Shake Hands?: Surviving in Another Culture*; *Journey to Jerusalem: Making a Difference in the Middle East*; *Is That You, God?: Responses to the Missions Call*; *Changed Hearts, Changed Lives: God's Love at Work Through Asia-Pacific Nazarenes*; and *City of Fear* (for older children).

FOREWORD

Since Argentina is my birthplace, I am especially drawn to reading Pat Stockett Johnston's book *Extreme Argentina*. The woman I know as Pat is a dedicated missionary, willing to serve where placed. She is an encourager, a gifted speaker, and a talented writer. Pat is a self-starter who finds new and efficient ways to accomplish a task. The Pat I know is diverse in her interests and excels in all she does. She is fun-loving and accepts her own limitations with humility and humor. Pat has had a rich impact on my life and ministry both personally and professionally.

When my husband and I arrived in the Middle East as missionaries for the Church of the Nazarene, Pat and her husband became our mentors as my husband prepared for the detailed job of academic dean for Eastern Mediterranean Nazarene Bible College. Pat's organizational skills enabled us to understand the system, goals, objectives, and parameters of the job at hand. Her kind hospitality and sensitivity of spirit guided us through some new and exciting days.

Pat and I immersed ourselves in speaking seminars and writing conferences. Pat is an encourager and a strengthening counterpart in ministry. Her sense of joy and amplitude of interests make her a creative and resourceful writer. She captivates the fine hues commonly overlooked by others. She finds stamina in overcoming the odds and secures her will to survive in the energizing Spirit of God in her life.

I have met many people who demonstrate fortitude and perseverance. Pat is one of them. She exhibits the grace of endurance and the rewards of faithful investment.

As you read the flowing narrative of *Extreme Argentina* you will breathe a fresh understanding of God's moving Spirit in Argentina through the writing of an incredibly gifted woman of God.

Rev. Norma L Brunson
Clinical Chaplain
Sisters of Mercy Health Center
Oklahoma City, Oklahoma

ONE
SURPRISE ENDING

"I tell you, I went down to Argentina with Extreme Nazarene 2008* just to be a work horse," said Judy Davis. "I was going to just get up in the morning, eat, work, eat again, and go to bed. I worked on the Bruno Radi Convention Center and found that very fulfilling. But God also had other plans for me. Our team leader announced we would be going by bus to visit another town in the area to help the local church reach out to its community. We were assigned to the town of Garin. The church in Garin met under the carport of a local family's house. I only say carport because it looked like the 'old'-style carports we used to have in the United States. I think maybe the church had about 10 members, including children. But it's been a long time since I felt God so close, and I knew He was there for everyone. I was blown away by the amount of love there. My tears are flowing now as I describe my experience.

Judy and Ashley Davis

"My team painted some houses in Garin (usually no bigger than a 10' x 12' room) and cleaned up its 'park,' which was really a field of weeds. We fed some people and just served as needed. It was so great. My 16-year-old daughter, Ashley, came with me; it was also a life-changing event for her.

"I should tell you that I don't speak a word of Spanish. But the love those precious people showered on me will never leave my heart. The thing that influenced me the most was meeting the people of Garin. I was so blessed to be shoved on that bus! I think if I'd been given the option I might not have gone to Garin, because I don't like change and I'm kind of a coward when it comes to getting involved in something I'm totally unsure of. I didn't understand how God could use me for His glory on this project. I'm *so* not perfect, didn't speak the language, and could be of no help in verbally ministering to people. But still God had faith in me. I still can't believe it. Just writing this helps me remember that no matter what I've done in the past, God has faith in me. I would go back to them in a heartbeat if the opportunity ever arrived."

Judy, like many participants, joined the Extreme Nazarene team to be a blessing. She didn't expect anything in return. Instead God blessed her in an amazing way. Read the following stories and learn how other Extreme Nazarene 2008 team members experienced God's miraculous touch during their adventure in Argentina.

*Learn more about future Extreme Nazarene projects at: www.extremenazarene.org.

TWO
GOD WILL TAKE CARE OF YOU

Not a missionary speaker! Jim Henderson shook his head in frustration. *How did I miss noticing that when I signed up for this date?* It was too late to cancel being a part of the Boise First Church Sunday morning's worship sound, lights, and media presentation team.

Growing up, Jim's dad purposefully established the listening-to-a-missionary-speaker pattern for his family when he'd say, "A missionary is scheduled to speak this Sunday. Let's skip church!" Like kids do, Jim picked up on his dad's negative attitude and, as an adult, avoided listening to missionary speakers whenever possible. He'd never enjoyed a single missionary message to date.

After taking his place in a pew, Jim discovered the speaker that morning would be Brent Deakins.* Brent was coming to share about the Extreme Nazarene project in Pilar, Argentina. Jim knew Brent was the son of Bob and Lyn Deakins—people his family had contact with during their few months at Boise First. *Being as I know his parents, I guess I'll give him the courtesy of listening,* he decided.

As Brent began to speak, Jim presumed it would be the same type of dry missionary message he'd heard before. Instead Brent asked his wife, Nicole, to the platform. She shared how God had changed her heart regarding material possessions. "I was willing to serve as a missionary with my husband—as long as I didn't have to give up my house. Finally, I was able to offer my house to God to support our missionary career. Soon afterward, God gave us the financial support we needed, and we were able to keep our home. That's the kind of God we have."

After Nicole finished speaking, Brent's Extreme Nazarene PowerPoint presentation impressed Jim. This project wasn't just about witnessing to people in faraway lands. Participants would also be involved in building the Bruno Radi Convention Center. This building would serve as a training center for pastors and lay people as well as an outreach facility for the community. *It would be interesting to serve in a project like this,* Jim acknowledged to himself, *but time and money issues stand in my way.*

Inside the Bruno Radi Convention Center

Next Brent explained the great need for construction workers to help finish the Center. He ended his appeal with these words: "We really need plumbers—especially a commercial plumber—in the worst way. Would plumbers in the audience please raise their hands?"

Jim shifted uncomfortably in his seat, for he worked as a commercial plumber. He focused on the people in the audience. *There's got to be another plumber somewhere in this congregation.* He kept scanning the crowd and waiting for other plumbers to raise their hands. None did. In what seemed like an eternity, Jim finally raised his hand.

The speaker thanked Jim and then told him, "You need to think about going to Argentina with us."

Jim spent the final minutes of that service considering his predicament. *How am I going to get out of this one?*

While Jim's family stood around after the service talking to friends in the foyer, his daughter Rebecca spoke to him. "Why don't you go talk to Brent, Dad?" she asked. "You'd be so good for this project."

"It sounds like fun," Jim replied, "but there are too many things standing in the way."

At that moment Joyce, one of the ladies who worked with Jim and Cheryl at the church's Upward basketball concession stand, approached Jim and said, "Aren't you a plumber?"

Jim shrugged. "Yes, I am."

"Well," Joyce continued, "I don't have plumber skills. But if you'll go, I'll pay for the cost of getting you there."

"I'm not a subtle kind of person," Jim shared later. "Just tell me what you want, and don't just hint around about it. God hit me right upside the head with a two-by-four with Joyce's words. God knew what kind of inspiration I needed, and Joyce was it."

After thanking Joyce, Jim realized he needed to talk to Brent face-to-face, so he turned around and went back into the sanctuary. He spotted Brent standing near the platform and hurried to catch him before he left. The words tumbled from his lips—words he never thought he'd say. "I'm the guy who raised his hand in this morning's worship service. I need to understand what being a part of the Argentina project means—what my job description would be and how much the trip will cost."

"A group of contractors and structural engineers plan to meet for breakfast next week to discuss the project," Brent said. "Why don't you join us?"

Sitting around that breakfast table, Jim wasn't sure how being involved in this missions project was going to play out. But he was impressed with the dimension of it and the excellent plans for the buildings. Finally he said, "I'm willing to go, but I don't see how I can swing it financially."

Much to Jim's surprise, the men started laughing. "If money is the only thing holding you back, don't worry," they said. "God will take care of it."

Although Jim had always believed that having faith was one of his strong spiritual areas, he says he learned a new lesson in obedience that day. "I realized I had to trust God a lot more than I ever had before. After much prayer, I recognized that God was leading me to go. Now I needed to make plans. I perceived a roadblock in front of each arrangement—an insurmountable problem that would be the deal-breaker that kept me home."

Jim and his wife, Cheryl, discussed Jim's participation in the project many times. Cheryl finally shared her struggle with him. "I trust God to cover your expense for the trip. But what about your family? Who's going to provide for our financial needs while you're gone?"

Although not knowing the answer to her questions, Jim approached his employer about taking time off from work to help with a missions project. "I didn't expect them to approve my request," Jim said. "I even anticipated losing my job if I decided to go. Not only did my boss give me the time off, several of my coworkers contributed several hundred dollars toward the cost of the trip. I was headed for Argentina!"

Jim continued, "It's amazing how God opened the doors that helped me finance my trip and provide for my family while I was gone. For example, photography is my hobby, so I'm always trolling the internet for good buys. I found a highly desirable lens and camera with a price far below market value. . . . Even though I wanted to keep the lens after I purchased the set, I resold both the camera and lens and used the profit to help finance my trip.

"While I was working . . . in Argentina, Cheryl E-mailed me some great news. "One of your relatives received your support letter and called me. "How much money is needed for Jim's trip?" he asked.

"I told him your entire trip has been funded, but that we still need $500 to help us with our living expenses. His $500 check arrived in the mail today!"

Jim has traveled to Argentina twice for Extreme Nazarene. The first time he helped organize the KidsZone project. In this project, the missions experience was geared toward kids and teenagers. The adults did construction and outreach with the children integrated into the program whenever possible.

On the second trip, Jim planned to be involved only with the construction phase. However he decided to participate in an outreach ministry at a church in Jaguel, a town south of Buenos Aires. "I wasn't very excited about going," Jim said, "but I thought it would give me a chance to take pictures of Pilar and the surrounding areas.

"During our group's three visits to the church, I found the people and their faith in God overwhelming. Although they had very few material possessions by [our] standards, they still praised God. The photos I took of the church members and neighborhood children who participated in the Vacation Bible School portray the joy and thankfulness expressed on their faces. To me, their actions represented a whole new dimension of what it means to follow Christ.

"My group also participated in Vacation Bible School classes and a worship service in a local park. The thankfulness expressed by the church members staggered me. I expected to give my talents and gifts to the folks of Pilar. I never expected them to bless me far beyond what I could give to them.

"During my participation in Extreme 2008, God taught me how to set priorities in my life—how to put Him first. My family's faith has been strengthened tremendously through my trips. They've seen God at work—how He provides for needs and opens doors to ministry.

"Are you feeling God's call to participate in the impossible? All of us have God-given skills or talents. If God is calling you to do something for Him, don't put barricades in the way. Trust God to take care of you. You won't regret it."

* Brent Deakins is the U.S.A. Mobilization Officer for Extreme Nazarene. You can contact Brent via E-mail at: b.deakins@extremenazarene.org.

THREE
HOPE CONQUERS ALL

When Brent Deakins came to share about the Extreme Argentina 2008 project at her church in Grangeville, Idaho, Lonna Vopat wasn't thinking about ministering to women in Argentina. She was completely involved in plans for a HOPE trip to Nigeria through her organization, In His Grace Ministries. "After my return from Nigeria, I met with Brent to discuss a women's outreach ministry for Extreme 2008," said Lonna. "I then accepted [the] invitation to visit the June 2007 KidsZone project to check out women's ministries opportunities. After I met the Argentine women on the Extreme Nazarene team, it took less than 24 hours for the Lord to prompt my heart and give me a vision for reaching Argentine women with the HOPE of Jesus Christ. The Lord immediately began dropping everything into place (as He always does), and I prayerfully moved ahead."

Three-fold Strategy for Women's Ministries

Lonna and Liz Dickson (director of the ministry Love UnVeiled) suggested that the Extreme Nazarene team use a three-fold strategy of leadership training, conferences, and impact ministries centered around the theme of HOPE *(Esperanza)*. The planned events for women would equip their Argentine sisters-in-Christ to share their faith, grow in their knowledge of Jesus, and deepen their understanding of who they are in Christ. "As the Extreme team began to plan the content for each outreach event, it became obvious that Lonna's background would enable her to play a major role in reaching the hearts of the women," said Brent Deakins. "Her story is a beautiful picture of God's redeeming grace."

"My story starts with my parents' divorce when I was 3," Lonna shared. "My mother got custody of my older bother and me. A year later my mother abandoned us, and we moved in with our father. Weekend visits began with my mother when I was 5. So did the sexual abuse by her live-in boyfriend.

"When I was 8, my father remarried. Unknown to my dad, his new wife was schizophrenic, and I suffered severe physical and emotional abuse for four years before my dad divorced her. After his divorce we moved to Idaho where I thought I would finally be able to live in safety and security. But I was haunted by my past.

"When I was 13 some friends took me to church, and I heard about Jesus. Later I attended a weekend Bible camp where I asked Him to be my Savior. In that moment I felt a love so big and so safe. When I returned to my non-Christian home, however, our enemy, Satan, told me I was unworthy of God's love. *You're used. You're defiled. You're dirty. God can't love you.*

"I believed Satan's lies and turned to drugs and alcohol to numb my pain and promiscuous behavior to find someone who cared. The amazing thing was that no one suspected I was living a miserable life because I wore a flawless mask that covered my pain. My years of molestation and abuse hung over my life like a dark shadow. After graduating from high school, I got involved with a drug-dealing ex-con who spoke the words I longed to hear: *I love you.* He showed his love with his fists and controlling, abusive behavior. I finally left that relationship and then discovered I was pregnant. I chose to abort the baby.

"At age 20 I had another abortion. Shortly afterward I came home from a night of partying but cold sober, thinking I had nothing left to live for. I loaded the gun a friend had given me for protection and sat alone sobbing in a heap on the floor, wondering how

I had fallen so low. As I raised the gun's cold barrel to my temple, I felt a hand on my shoulder. I knew it was the hand of Jesus. I had a decision to make. I could either pull the trigger and end it all, or I could drop the gun and grab His hand. I dropped the gun and grasped the hope of Jesus Christ. He literally lifted me from the floor and embraced me. I asked for His forgiveness and promised to serve Him with my life. I will never forget His reply: 'I have been waiting for you. Welcome home, daughter.' When I sat that gun down, I walked into a new life, forgiven and restored—all because of God's grace."

Lonna began surrounding herself with Christian friends. Eventually she met and married Kevin Vopat. In 2002 Lonna won the Mrs. Idaho pageant and represented Idaho in the Mrs. America pageant. She never dreamed God would use both her abusive childhood and her reign as Mrs. Idaho to open doors for her to tell women all over the world about God's love for them.

Extreme 2008 Events for Women

During the Extreme 2008 events for women, Lonna shared her testimony at a shelter for abused women, women's prisons, and women's conferences.

The following stories of God's grace and the power of hope during those events will warm your heart.

Women's Maximum Security Prison

Forty-five Extreme Nazarene women volunteers boarded the bus one hot Tuesday morning, headed for the Ezezia women's maximum security prison Block 31 in Buenos Aires. Myriam Pozzi, who works in the South America Nazarene regional office in Pilar, arranged the visit through SACDEM. This organization, run by former convicts Daniel and Mariaelene Ruffinati, had worked in women's prisons in Argentina for over 25 years. Here are some sobering statistics concerning the women prisoners:

- Ninety percent were convicted of drug trafficking.
- Over 80 percent had children on the outside. A majority had more than one child.
- Thirty-five percent were foreigners. If drug traffickers are caught in Argentina, they do their time there.
- Eighty percent had suffered some type of physical and/or sexual abuse in their lives.

Everyone expected a regular, controlled prison visit with little contact with the inmates because of security concerns. "However, the impossible happened," said Lonna. "The Extreme group received permission to have a pampering session just like the one we'd held the day before in a women's minimum security prison. That meant we would be allowed to do hand, foot, and shoulder massages and lavish aromatic creams and love on the prisoners. Then we were told the administration planned to have both cell blocks attend our meeting together. Sometimes they didn't mix the two blocks' inmates due to rival gang fighting. But the warden told Ruffinati if they didn't allow both blocks to attend the meeting, the women who got to come would be targeted and later hurt by the other block. We alerted the Extreme gals to this, and though visibly nervous, they didn't back out of the visit.

"Security was tight when the bus arrived. Two guards came on board to inspect the bus and us before we were allowed to enter the prison. After we passed inspection the guards led us into the recreation room. Its few, small windows were placed 10 feet above the floor, thus allowing for little ventilation. The plus 100-degree room temperature was stifling. As the group of 137 prisoners entered the room, some recognized the people from SACDEM (who visit this prison twice a week) and the mood lightened. Inmates ran to hug and greet people they clearly knew and trusted. They'd come to the room to see a program they knew SACDEM had arranged for them to attend.

"Soon 'spa' stations—each manned by two to three Extreme women—were set up, and the inmates were invited to choose a seat and be pampered. One Extreme visitor massaged shoulders, another hands, and the third feet—often at the same time. Each massage lasted 10 to 15 minutes. Most of the women wept as the Extreme gals pampered them. They weren't used to being touched with no other purpose than to share Jesus' love. None of them had ever had their feet massaged. They were astounded that strangers would come in and treat them so kindly. Slowly the facial expressions changed, tears flowed, and the inmates softened as we visitors tried to communicate in English, Spanish, and sign language."

During the spa time, Sara—a young German woman who spoke fluent English—began to share her story with Liz Dickson. Sara had only been at Ezezia one week. She didn't speak Spanish and was completely overwhelmed by this prison environment. She had grown up in a Catholic home, but married a man who beat her and tried to involve her in his drug business. For three years Sara resisted getting involved in the drug trade despite abuse that included such things as cigarette burns, the scars of which were apparent on her arms.

"During Christmas last year," Sara said, "I adopted a cat. I gave it all my affection. One night my husband grabbed the cat and started to scalp him before my eyes. He threatened to kill my pet unless I agreed to help him carry drugs to Argentina. I was terrified and worn down from the years of abuse, so I agreed. My husband and I were arrested when we arrived at the Buenos Aires airport." Sara talked and cried and prayed the sinner's prayer even before the presentation by Lonna. That helped to set the mood for what was to come. When the spa time ended, the inmates pulled their seats together and clapped to the contemporary worship music being played.

After a short prayer, Lonna shared her personal story of neglect, abandonment, and abuse during childhood. She told about living through drug abuse, her countless harmful choices, and the consequences of living a godless lifestyle. As Lonna reached the focal point of her talk and prepared to move into the time for the women's responses, the sound system went crazy.

"It resembled shrieks, or screams—not like any sound I'd ever heard before," said Cristina Pacheco, who as a singer was familiar with normal microphone feedback. "It seemed like an attack by demons." Cristina and the other Extreme women formed a hedge around the inmates and began to pray. Lonna raised her voice loud enough to be heard across the room: "I will not stop speaking until each one of you has heard about the Savior, Jesus Christ!" The inmates erupted in applause. After several minutes the noise abated and Lonna continued speaking: "You are no different than me. God loves you despite the mistakes you have made. In fact, we are all sinners who can be saved through God's grace." Lonna ended her testimony by saying, "Is there anyone here who wants to ask Jesus to come into her heart and be the Lord of her life?" All but 5 of the 137 inmates and the guards stood and joined in the sinner's prayer. The Extreme team was overwhelmed and praised God for the incredible response.

Toward the end of the visit, Lonna and other team members talked and prayed with many tearful inmates as they responded to the Spirit's call. The visit ended with mixed groups of prisoners and visitors sharing sandwiches and soft drinks. The Church of the Nazarene in Grangeville, Idaho, had prepared 600 fabric bags for the inmates and filled them with shampoo, lotion, a toothbrush, toothpaste, a brush, comb, and a washcloth. Every prisoner received a bag as they filed out of the room, many with tears streaming down their faces. The guards unexpectedly allowed the inmates to take bottles of soft drinks back to their cells. The prison guards, who were mostly women, also received care bags.

Daniel then received permission for Lonna to go deep into the prison to visit the cell blocks of women who didn't attend the meeting. "We visited two cell blocks that contained young offenders between 18 and 20 years of age who weren't allowed to mingle with the older inmates because of their age and vulnerability," said Lonna. "The oppression was tangible. We approached a cell holding four young, teenaged girls. They looked hardened beyond their young years. Two of them had large tattoos covering their arms. They were excited to see Daniel and Mariaelene and reached their hands out of the bars to hold their hands and to shake ours.

"After a brief visit we moved to the next cell. The four residents there looked similar except for one—a girl in pink sweatpants and a white tank top. She was tall and thin and looked strikingly similar to my niece, who is 16 years old. Her big brown eyes and delicate features struck me. The fear in those brown eyes spoke volumes, without a word being uttered. She was shy and didn't approach the bars with the other girls. Finally she came up and made eye contact with me. I smiled and she smiled. I reached out to take her hand and she reciprocated. All I could think was that this beautiful young girl should be picking out a party dress or having slumber parties. The tears welled in both our eyes. When the guards told us it was time to move on, I wanted to wrap that girl in my arms and tell her everything was going to be OK. But all I could do was tell her Jesus loved her and that I would be praying for her. It wasn't until we walked out of the sweltering prison block and heard the security doors loudly clanging behind us that I was able to take a full breath. The darkness in the prisons was truly suppressing. I can't imagine living in those conditions on a daily basis."

Cynthia Onthank, the photographer for In His Grace Ministries, was the only member of the team allowed to take a digital camera and video equipment into the prison. She was given unlimited access to record the events of the day. Members of the SAC-DEM team said the warden had never allowed that freedom in their 25 years of ministry in the prison. "What I remember and am grateful for is that I could record the tears of pain and the tears of joy," said Cynthia. "I was amazed at how the inmates enjoyed posing with friends for pictures, just like a group of women outside prison. They wanted prints, which I couldn't give them, but I let them view their pictures on my digital camera screen. If nothing else, my camera made them smile and forget their troubles for a few minutes."

The women who made decisions for Christ were followed up by SACDEM during their weekly visits. At least a few Bibles are available in the prison in English, Russian, and Spanish. But new Christians are threatened by a group of inmates who wear an ominous tattoo of a figure called "Saint of Death." When women come to know the Lord, this group of self-proclaimed Satanists put witchcraft items around the new believers' beds to cause fear and intimidation. We all need to pray for the new believers' safety, for their release at the right time so they can be removed from the prison atmosphere, and that women like Sara will not be sucked back into the kind of life from which prison may actually have been God's plan to help her escape.

Women's Conferences

The Extreme Nazarene 2008 team planned two women's conferences. Both conferences were named *Esperanza Argentina*, which means Argentina Hope. Fifteen hundred women attended the first conference, and 1,200 women attended the second conference. Both venues were in Buenos Aires. Women from all walks of life attended the conferences: pastors' wives, government officials, women of affluence, drug addicts, former prostitutes, and women from the barrios (slums).

Cristina Pacheco, from San Diego, began the evening with an amazing time of worship. Next it was Lonna's turn to share. "As I prepared to speak at the women's conferences, I asked the Lord to reveal His message for the evening to me. I'd been told that, culturally, Argentine women were focused on their appearance, and that some women starved themselves to look good. In fact, an Argentine supermodel died of anorexia only months before the conference. Dressing fashionably is also culturally important. My experience in the Mrs. America pageant had opened my eyes to the length women will go to obtain physical perfection and the opportunity to be 'someone' in the world's eyes—even if it's only for 15 minutes.

"After much prayer, I felt that some material from my presentation 'From Maybelline to the Maker' would be appropriate for Argentine women. The audience was shocked when I walked onto the stage wearing heavy make-up and a tiara on my head. The women watched in amazement as I began to remove the false eyelashes, the make-up, and the jewelry I wore to make myself beautiful. I discarded my crown last. 'God wants us to be real,' I said. 'He loves the real us. The only crown worth winning is the one offered by God when we ask His forgiveness. You can choose to live as a daughter of Jesus. He will create in you an inner beauty that will last.'"

At the end of Lonna's talk, many women kneeled at the altar to commit their lives to Jesus and begin their walk with Him. Following a time of prayer, the conferees watched *Magdalena: Released from Shame*, a new film for women distributed through JESUS Film Harvest Partners. "The Church of the Nazarene has standing permission to use the *JESUS* film, any version, any language," Lonna said. "But the Spanish translation for *Magdalena* had not been completed. Campus Crusade [for Christ] truly bent over backward to get the film to us, and we only received it three weeks prior to the conference through God's amazing hand. The focus of the film is to help the *women of the world recognize their value in the eyes of Christ* . . .

"At the conclusion of the first conference, a woman came weeping down to the altar to pray. At the end of her prayer she told me her 22-year-old son had died of HIV only a month earlier. My heart broke. 'I'd been very angry at God for taking his life,' the woman said, 'but tonight I was able to let go of the anger and come back into God's arms.' I held her and prayed with her. As she left the venue that night she had a smile on her face, and we could see peace reflected in her countenance. It was incredible. Jesus had touched her, and her healing had begun.

"A group of women from the domestic abuse shelter we visited earlier that week attended the second conference. During that visit our team had pampered them by rubbing lotion into their hands and feet, moisturizing their faces, and painting their fingernails and toenails. They were amazed that we would do that for them. You could see the walls breaking down around those women's hearts. The women ranged in age from 18 to 54.

"After the pampering time I shared with the group of 19 women about how God had redeemed me and restored my life. When I finished my testimony, I asked if anyone wanted to ask Jesus into their heart. Two women raised their hands. The Holy Spirit prompted my heart to meet with each woman separately, so we paired our team members with a shelter resident. I moved around the room and sat with each shelter woman and her 'Extreme sister,' and we prayed for her. After praying with each wom-

Praying with grief-stricken women

an, the Holy Spirit moved hearts and every shelter resident made a decision to ask Jesus to be her Savior. We praised God for His touch that day.

"One young woman's story especially touched my heart. At only 18 years of age she had a 6-week-old baby boy. Both she and her son had been diagnosed with HIV. Her pain was tangible. She was angry at God and very scared for her son's life. As we shared with her God's gift of grace and eternal life she began to cry. We told her that HIV was not their death sentence, but that God had a plan for her life and for the life of her son. She cried and cried and then said, 'I want this eternal life. And I want my son to have it too.' We prayed the salvation prayer with her, and [we] could see an immediate change in her. Her smile radiated, and the fear was gone. We witnessed God's amazing power to transform a life right before our eyes."

Lonna testifies to the Lord's healing power. "Today I live as a restored, redeemed, and uplifted woman because of Jesus in my life. Years ago, if I had written my greatest dream for my life, it wouldn't compare to what God has done for me. God loves me so much. He wrote my story, and I get to live it. God has an adventure for everyone. He's waiting to share the story He's written for you. All you have to do is ask."

Lonna Vopat now ministers to women and children full-time through In His Grace Ministries, an organization that reaches out to women around the world through discipleship and evangelism. The vision of In His Grace Ministries is to see women encouraged to find their identity in Jesus Christ, empowered to live the authentic Christian life, and mobilized to share the message of hope with women at home and abroad. She speaks at national Christian conferences, ladies' retreats, special events, and university campuses.

You can learn more about In His Grace Ministries at www.in-his-grace.com.

FOUR
DISCOVERING GOD'S NEW ASSIGNMENT

"Our assignment in Pilar, Argentina, began in 2006 when Eric Seaney, pastor of our Nazarene church in Kuna, Idaho, asked my husband and me to make a trip to Argentina," said Judy Turley. "We joined other Extreme Nazarene representatives to plan a time for families to participate in the 2007 KidsZone . . . experience. Our exposure to the wonderful Argentine people and the area in and around Pilar was invaluable in helping us design activities for parents and children of all ages. After we returned to Kuna, God enabled us to put together a team of 17 people who pledged to return to Argentina for the summer 2007 KidsZone project. Our church also sponsored Pastor Eric, his wife, Mindi, and their three children.

"When we arrived in Pilar for Kid's Zone 2007 with our Kuna church team, we received our local church assignment: to support and mentor a newly formed home church in a barrio named Garin. Carlos and Robin Radi were our interpreters. They shared a short history about Pastor Bruno, the Garin pastor with us that evening.

"At birth, Bruno's father named him after his friend Bruno Radi (who was Carlos Radi's father). As the South America Regional director, Bruno Radi had the privilege of discipling his young namesake years later. As an unmarried, 27-year-old man, Pastor Bruno had a passion for evangelism and discipleship. He had led a man named Sergio to the Lord nine months prior to our team's arrival. Sergio's wife, Vicky, and their whole family also committed their lives to the Lord. Sergio was now being discipled by Pastor Bruno to pastor this newly formed barrio church in Garin.

"The next morning we each grabbed a brown-bag lunch and boarded an old Greyhound bus and waited while tools, wheelbarrows, and paint were stowed in the luggage compartment under the bus. About 50 minutes later our team arrived in Garin. The church had been meeting on Sergio and Vicky's patio each week. Their patio had no roof, and the walls of the patio needed paint. After introductions and a time of prayer and praise, the equipment was unloaded from the bus, and construction began on the much-needed roof.

"A few members of the team invented games to play with children nearby. Other team members went door-to-door with Pastor Bruno handing out flyers inviting neighborhood children to [Vacation Bible School] to be held later that day. Little did I know that this trek around the Garin barrio with Pastor Bruno would later on turn out to be a turning point in my own life.

"In Garin there are no doorbells. Pastor Bruno would stand outside the gate and clap his hands. Immediately half a dozen barking dogs would announce our arrival. At one home, after the clapping-and-dogs-barking approach, an older lady named Dalya slowly limped to the gate. She looked weary and beaten down. Pastor Bruno began to speak to her in Spanish. Within about five minutes, he put his hands on her weary-laden shoulders and began to pray. I don't speak Spanish, but I knew he was praying for her salvation; you could sense the presence of the Holy Spirit descend on her. Pastor Bruno proceeded to give her an invitation to Vacation Bible School.

"We continued around the neighborhood that afternoon, following that same pattern. Clapping of hands. Barking dogs. A greeting. An invitation. Later that day about 50 children gathered on the church patio for puppets, songs, and a salvation message.

"The next day a few of us had the privilege of walking the dirt roads of Garin with Pastor Bruno again. Several families invited us into their homes. Pastor Bruno would easily and gently laugh and talk, and then within a few minutes he would begin to share Jesus. Many accepted Jesus on the spot.

"On Sunday Dalya and several other new converts attended the little 'roofed' patio church. Through an interpreter, we learned Dalya's story. She had accepted Jesus as her Savior that day when Pastor Bruno prayed for her at the gate. She was a grandmother raising two young grandsons, she was sick, and she needed prayer for healing. Sunday was a praise and worship service that few of us will forget; it was a service that reached the portals of heaven. I'm sure the angels were rejoicing!

"Upon returning to the [United States], I experienced a restlessness I couldn't explain. Something new was beginning to take shape in my heart. My adventure [in Argentina] led me to reflect on several areas in my own life—most importantly evangelism and discipleship. I saw in Bruno Radi, and his namesake Bruno, a relationship close to that of Paul and Timothy. I began to study the life of Jesus and His primary investment in 12 men. The Lord began to show me I was spreading myself too thin in my ministries. Instead, I intentionally needed to spend more time with fewer of 'God-chosen' people.

"As I watched Pastor Bruno in action sharing his concern for lost people, it began to dawn on me that I couldn't be content to be just a silent witness of Jesus' love. Today finds me more deliberate in my investment in the people God puts in my path, always watching for a potential Timothy in whom I can speak boldly and invest in deeply. I truly did receive a new assignment from God because of my adventure."

FIVE
ALL IN THE FAMILY

The sun shone brightly that January day as the Extreme Nazarene 2008 Hostetler/Lynch church plant team drove out of the Seminario Teologico Nazareno Del Cono Sur compound in Pilar, Argentina. Dr. Mike Poe, a professor at Northwest Nazarene University, was included in the group. They had a target destination: the Villa Devoto neighborhood park, located on the edge of Buenos Aires. Even though most of the group had a limited knowledge of Spanish, Mike wasn't worried. *I can do this, even if my Spanish is limited to short phrases like* buenos dias *and* buenos noches. *I can pass out flyers to family groups gathered in the park that invite their children to a puppet show.*

Once they arrived at the park, the team broke into smaller groups. The local church kids assigned to

Mike's group rushed ahead, leaving the pastors who were translating for the group behind. The children soon surrounded a large family group and insisted everyone take a flyer. "We're putting on a wonderful puppet show later this afternoon," they explained. "Come and join us!"

The kids must have told the family that some visitors from the United States were helping to hand out flyers, because one of the men waited for the group to catch up. He pointed to himself and proclaimed, "Omar." Then he pointed to Mike and asked, "California?"

Mike shook his head no then said, "Idaho." From the blank look on everyone's faces, it was obvious this group had never heard of the state of Idaho or its potatoes.

Omar continued to ask Mike short questions in English, followed by, "How I doing?" Mike always replied, "Great!" all the while hoping a translator would arrive.

Omar received great satisfaction from his ability to communicate. He'd turn to his family with a big grin and state, "*Si!* Great!"

Mike and Omar shook hands several times during their question-and-answer session. Eventually Omar pulled out a small, gold-enameled medallion that hung on a gold chain around his neck and announced, "*Chacarita* best!"

Thinking it was an emblem for a local soccer team, Mike responded, "Yeah, the best!"

Later someone explained to Mike that Omar was a member of the *Hincha Chacarita*, the most violent soccer hooligan gang in the area. Recently the gang's members had closed down a large expressway with their rioting. "I hate to think about what would have happened if I'd responded negatively when Omar first said, '*Chacarita* best!'" Mike said later.

Pastor Carlos from the local church and Pastor Arturo from Bakersfield, California, noticed the noisy gathering and quickly came to check out what was happening. Pastor Carlos started talking to Omar; Mike could tell from his limited knowledge of Spanish that the conversation was about Jesus. After a very short time, tears spilled from Omar's eyes and down his cheeks as he listened to the pastor's words.

Mike rarely carried a handkerchief, but that day he pulled one out of his pocket. "Take this," he whispered to Omar. After wiping his face, Omar returned the damp cloth with a quiet "*Gracias*." Soon Omar bowed his head, prayed for forgiveness, and began his journey with Jesus.

Meanwhile, Pastor Arturo began to witness to Omar's son-in-law, Fernando, a young man in his early 20s. "Accept Jesus as your Savior, my friend, and find a new way of living." Fernando quickly responded to the Spirit's nudging and turned his life over to Christ. Next Omar's daughter Giselle responded to the invitation to a new way of life.

During this time, Paula, Omar's other daughter, stood just on the edge of the action. Soon she, too, joined Omar in accepting the Lord. "When Pastor Carlos, Pastor Arturo, and Mike started talking to us," Paula later explained, "I noticed Mike's bass voice. I liked listening to him talk, even though I don't speak English. I felt a peace in those three men I didn't understand . . . but that I liked."

Pastor Arturo praying with Omar and his daughter Paula

Before the puppet show began, Omar said, "I have a request, Pastor Carlos." He spoke with a pleading tone. "My son-in-law Marcelo is a drug addict. Would you please talk to him about accepting Jesus as Lord?" Omar pulled his cell phone out of his pocket. "I'll call him right now."

Shortly afterward Pastor Carlos was explaining who he was to Marcelo. The pastor invited him to join his wife, Giselle, and family at the puppet show that afternoon.

In the meantime, Omar's wife sat a little way from the group, acting like she was paying no attention to the activity going on around the gringo strangers. Finally she approached the group. Pastor Carlos immediately began witnessing directly to her, and she chose to follow Jesus as well.

The time for the puppet show arrived, and the group dispersed. Marcelo, the drug-addict son-in-law, came to the park, and after the puppet show he, too, accepted Christ as his Savior.

The next Sunday the Extreme Nazarene group headed once again to the Villa Devoto Park. Soon Omar's daughters, Giselle and Paula; their husbands, Fernando and Marcelo; and their children arrived for the day's activities.

"Where's Omar?" someone asked. "He's coming. But he wants to know if Mike is here today," the family replied. "Now we can call and tell him yes!"

With the help of Pastor Arturo, Mike spent the morning communicating with Fernando. He was the most outgoing of the family and asked the most questions. Mike learned that Fernando was also a teacher, and the two educators connected on another level.

When Omar arrived, everyone laughed as they watched Mike greet him with a hug and traditional kisses on the cheeks. As Pastor Arturo translated for the two men, Omar mentioned he liked boxing and struck a boxer's pose. Pastor Arturo assured him that Jesus would help him fight off the devil.

Omar's face filled with excitement as he asked, "Can you take a picture of Pastor Arturo, Mike, and me fighting off the devil?" The men stood, fists up, for that photo.

Who would believe that puppets at a park could lead to a grandfather, a grandmother, two daughters, and two sons-in-law accepting Jesus as their Savior? And who can predict how homes full of Jesus' love will affect the grandchildren? All Mike can say is, "God is at work. He's calling people to himself. And Extreme 2008 made that connection possible—in a park."

SIX
WHEN A LOSS IS A WIN

"When my husband, Tom, and I got married 22 years ago, we had great plans to become missionaries and save the world," said Robin Watters. "We went to the Nazarene Theological Seminary in Kansas City for a few years, and then both of us ended up working in the medical field in the United States. Are we currently on the mission field? I'd like to think so, even though we don't live in Africa. You may wonder how we could feel like missionaries when we live in Nampa, Idaho—one of the Church of the Nazarene's 'Mecca' cities.

"Six years ago we slowly answered a call to help plant a church in Nampa called Real Life Community Church of the Nazarene. At the time we were attending Nampa First Church of the Nazarene, which is a large church with lots of activities for all ages.

The hardest thing about leaving Nampa First Church was our concern for our four precious children. We finally concluded that starting a church plant could be similar to being a missionary, as missionaries often lack resources for their children when living overseas, yet God provides for them. We decided to trust God with our children.

"One of the most prominent ways God provided was through Arnie Ytreeide, another church planter. He mentored our son Troy in video filming and editing while he completed 7th through 12th grade. Arnie is now Troy's Northwest Nazarene University professor. He continues to nurture our son's passion for filming while Troy works on his mass communications degree. As you will see, Troy's video knowledge led him and us to the mission field.

"What does all this have to do with Argentina? The song 'Step by Step' comes to mind as I share this story. As we've worked at the Real Life Church these past six years, our lives have changed immensely. We only live three miles from our previous church, but in a whole different world. The ratios are switched from most people knowing and growing in Christ, along with a few new believers, to most people attending our church being either nonbelievers or new believers with only a handful of seasoned Christians. The majority of attendees have no idea who God is.

"I will never forget sitting in the local Moxie Java coffee shop with my friend Jodi, who'd just been baptized at our church family camp. I noticed she was holding her new red Bible, so I casually asked her, 'What do you know about the Bible?'

"She slowly flipped the book open and stared at a page. 'I've never really read the Bible,' she finally replied.

"I was shell-shocked. That was only the beginning for my husband and me as we met and lived our lives around people with little or no church background. We left our comfortable church zone, learned a new culture, and fell in love with people [who] have few masks, little money, and complicated lives. They are beautiful. They love and want God with such earnest sincerity.

"I think this experience must resemble that of missionaries who travel to a new country and work in a new culture. They set out to teach the people, and in the process the people teach them. At times the ministry overwhelms us as we realize the spiritual needs of our community. And yes, we even feel frustrated as we recognize the spiritual wealth of established churches nearby. But then I must remember establishment is not our goal. Our mission is to touch others with Christ so that they may have a chance to live their lives with Him.

"In 2003, when our son Troy was 14 years old, he was asked to go to Ukraine and film a . . . project. We didn't know it at the time, but that project documented the birth of the Extreme Nazarene Ministries organization. My husband and I also joined Troy's . . . team. We experienced an amazing trip, and during that three-week period fell in love with the Ukrainians.

"Participation in the Ukraine project was a life-changing trip, as I believe all mission trips have the capacity to be. That trip gave us a dream to take all four of our children on a missions trip before they moved away from home, because we could see the love of missions that trip placed in our young son's heart. In the back of my mind I wondered how we could ever financially make this happen, since just getting a family vacation squeaked out of the budget took careful planning. We gave God our dream.

"Along came the Extreme Nazarene 2008 project in Pilar, Argentina. News of the project immediately caught our interest, but we hung on the fringe, knowing finances were a large obstacle. Then, at age 18, Troy decided he was ready to start making some of his own decisions. He signed up for the project without even talking to us about it. At first I was fearful, realizing college started in the fall for him. Then I realized that if he was going to be making his own decisions, this was one a mother really couldn't gripe about. Troy's memory was much better than ours as he reminded us of how God had helped us finance our Ukraine trip.

"A few weeks before the Argentina project deadline, Brian Tibbs sent us a scholarship form from an anonymous donor who was willing to financially help families wanting to go to Argentina. Much to our surprise and delight, we received a scholarship acceptance letter that stated the only condition was that all four family members listed on the form go to Argentina. So Troy, Tara, Kurt, and I headed to Argentina. It was too late in the summer for Tom to get off work, so he and our youngest daughter, Kelly, didn't apply. But they were able to support us greatly with their prayers and encouragement.

"Troy and I were assigned to a medical team that [ministered] to Argentine Indians in several rural areas. I remember the first meeting with the other medical team members. I thought we were an odd mix of people and backgrounds, and I wondered how it would all work out. Then Harry, a retired career missionary, shared about his life as a missionary in a rural African region. I could feel the Spirit of the Lord drawing us all together as a team.

"We left the next evening on a small bus for a planned 16-hour bus ride that took 20 hours. I can't recall ever laughing that much over such a long period of time, for once we became delirious from sitting in the same spot for hours with our knees crunched up under our chins, everything seemed funny.

"Of course our first patient was one of us! A large container fell off the top storage area in the bus onto Harry's bald head. We frantically searched for and found our first-aid kit. One of our pictures commemorates our first patient wearing his blue Band-Aid. We were grateful that it didn't seem to affect his great interpreting skills.

"We finally arrived in Formosa and traveled each day to a different clinic. Let me describe those clinics: they were located in a shack with a dirt floor, with chickens running between our feet as we treated patients. Many days patients walked for several hours to get to one of our clinics. I remember one day in particular when we noticed a large well full of black water near the clinic. I figured the water was for the animals. Later in the day I saw a little boy dipping a large container into the well. 'Who's that

Unsafe drinking water well

water for?' I asked. 'My community drinks this water,' he replied.

"Another day a lady brought in a large bag of oranges. She seemed so happy to share with us; she wasn't even wearing shoes. But she was giving oranges to us, even though we were there to give to her. That's how missions trips usually work. They backfire! You go to give and end up receiving.

"One scene I will always remember. Troy and I were walking down a dirt path toward a little church for an evening meeting after our amazing medical trip to [one of] those remote places. Suddenly he asked, 'Mom, how effective is the Kennedy salvation plan?' (We'd heard quite a bit about [this] evangelism plan from some Argentine church members.) We discussed the contrast between our current church back home that focuses so much on relationships. We talked about how powerful it would be to combine the two ways of evangelism.

"As we were standing in front of this little white church we could hear some young men playing soccer down the road. Kelsey, a young college girl on our medical team, said, 'Wow, I'd love to play a game of soccer right now.' We encouraged her to 'make a deal' with the boys: if we beat them at soccer, they would have to come to the church service with us. We could hear the boys' laughter clear down the road as Kelsey struggled in broken Spanish and sign language to explain 'the deal.'

"They accepted our offer, so we played an incredible soccer game on that bumpy dirt field. I felt like we played like a pro —well, almost. I *am* 42 years old!

"Did we win? Yes and no! Even though we lost the game, all eight boys still came to church, sat on the front row, and listened as the pastor preached. Several Argentines and Americans also testified as to how God had worked in their lives. It was one of the

Praying with one of the soccer boys

most beautiful church services I have ever attended. At the end of the meeting the pastor gave an altar call. Every soccer player was given the salvation plan and prayed with, and several of the boys accepted Christ as their Savior. We may have lost the soccer game, but we won at evangelism!

"We love the mission field, whether it be in our own backyard, Ukraine, or Argentina. We want others to know about God, about how much He loves them, and how He wants to walk daily with them. How do we do that? By entering their world and walking with them, just as Jesus enters our world and walks with us."

SEVEN
BAND-AIDS AND MOTORCYCLES SAVE THE DAY

When the Extreme Nazarene 2008 planners decided to establish various churches around the Bruno Radi Convention Center building project in Pilar, Argentina, members of Pastor Neil Horner's American team from Indiana, California, Idaho, and Oregon didn't know what they were in for. People from various church plant sites shared about the many highs and lows of planting a new church in Argentina. From those stories, Neil's team realized that no matter what happened at their site, they needed to be flexible and adaptable. "My team had the attitude of, 'Give us the tools, and we'll get it done,'" Neil said. "However, that desire didn't always mean that needed tools would be available on time or in the same shape that we used in the United States." The need to be flexible stands out in this report of God's ability to meet the needs of Neil's team.

"As the 20 or so of us who settled into the Hurlingham church plant team gathered on the first Sunday, we didn't have any notion of what to expect," said Neil. "The bus dropped us off at the house whose garage served as the current meeting place for church meetings. The home belonged to Pastor Roberto's mother. Our arrival in the early afternoon allowed time for the team to relax and get acquainted with each other and some of the Argentines.

"Pastor Roberto, Brian Utter, and I drove to the community project site where we would work later that week. Next we visited the plaza where we planned to show [the film] *From the Dark*. The movie portrays the life of Felix Vargas, a former warlord with [a] Colombian drug cartel whose life changed directions when he decided to follow Jesus.

"In Argentina plazas are parks where people in the neighborhood gather for various reasons. The first plaza we went to was located just a few blocks from the garage meeting place. It turned out to be a drug hangout. When we first cased the area in the middle of the afternoon, no one was around. However, when we came back with the team later that evening, a drug dealer sat in his car, radio blasting.

He got out and leaned over the top of his car, anticipating a sale. After we completed our setup, he finally left because he realized we were a lost cause as far as a sales went.

"We pulled the generator that would power the computer, the sound system, and the film projector out of the bus. When it was running, the generator made a roaring, rasping sound, but we had one extension cord that would allow us to place it a distance away. Eventually someone asked about the key to the generator. No one in our group had it. We called back to the central compound, but they didn't have the key either. Here we are, people arriving in response to all the invitations we'd handed out in all the side streets of town inviting people to come and watch a movie. And we can't start the generator.

"We tried to hot-wire the generator, but it was a sealed unit. We already had people praying for our outreach movie presentation; now we had more to pray about. We looked at the gazebo lights hanging above us to see if we could tap into them, but they'd been direct-wired into the street light. Before long, some of the neighbors got involved when a guy stepped up and said we could run a cord to his house.

"But we needed more than our one extension cord. Another neighbor brought some from his house. We ran the cords across a street and up the sidewalk to the house of this guy who had no idea what kind of movie we planned to show; he just knew we were from a church. When we finally got all the equipment hooked up to the neighbor's outlet, we turned on the generator. Nothing happened. We had no power.

"We began to backtrack all the connections and finally figured out the problem was the outlet in the house. Someone needed to stand there and hold the cord at the proper angle. We found some duct tape to hold the cord in place. We had power, and we were ready to start the show. During all of this preparation time, and then during the movie, two dogs chased each other between people and kids. In the midst of all the chaos, people heard the message of Christ and came to accept Him as their Savior. In the middle of all the nonsense, God was working. Since we chose to not give up and let Satan win, lives were changed that night.

"God must have figured that we could handle more, for all this was practice for what was to follow. The following Thursday was our work day at the construction site for the adult Down's Syndrome school.

We had other people join our Hurlingham plant team for the day.

"The children in our team had prepared a musical presentation, so they, their parents, and the Brazilian teens led by Pastor Anna had mime dramas ready to perform. Ten to 15 people stayed at the construction site to paint, while all the others were dropped off at the central plaza to begin canvassing. This plaza was in the center of town. Many people were outside that day—the kids on the playground while their parents relaxed. I noticed that almost all of the kids were accompanied by both parents. It was truly a family event to go to the plaza. Things are going along just great so far—great potential for sharing the gospel, great numbers of people, great plaza for the film setup. However, it's a good thing that our confidence wasn't in ourselves or the equipment.

"After the previous Sunday's experience, we made sure we had all the necessary equipment with us. Timing was crucial this night because we were adding two more events with the kids and the teens. We knew exactly how much time we needed for their music and dramas because we knew what time the sun would set. We wouldn't start the movie until dark, but we didn't want to lose the attention of those in the plaza with a big lag time between the live performances and the movie. So we planned a carefully-thought-out timeline. Part of the plan always included surrounding the plaza area with prayer warriors. Looking back, we realize the importance of this.

"At the plaza we set up all the equipment [and] hooked up all the electronic wiring and the lighting over the screen. Then we started the generator. Great—we had quiet power and a clear picture on the screen. We were ready! Except when we put the CD in for the kids' music and the Brazilians' mimes we had no sound. We changed cords and rechecked all the connections. Finally we found a headset from an iPod, plugged it into the projector, and heard music! We took cords from a couple of different pieces of equipment and cut the cords for the sound speakers to make the right connection for the audio to be heard. Since we couldn't find any tape, we literally used a couple Band-Aids to hold those connections together. You could hear our sigh of relief. The program could begin.

"We still had enough sunlight for the performers' faces to be seen. The younger kids performed admirably. The crowd clapped and hollered its approval. The teens, all in costume, were next on the program. But an unexpected cloud suddenly moved in. Soon after the teens started their performance, Pastor Anna gave me a disappointed look. I realized the teens' faces weren't visible, so people were going to miss the total effect of the mimes. We had no other lights to hang and no large flashlights. I felt so bad.

"Wait a minute. Earlier two guys had driven up on motorcycles. I spoke no Spanish, but I walked over to them, and through my motions they understood my request. They moved their bikes to face the performers, turned on the headlights, and sat there moving the handlebars to achieve a spotlight effect. They took turns highlighting each performer. Those guys also stayed and watched the entire Vargas film. They might not have stayed if we hadn't involved them.

"A lesson to be learned? Why are we amazed when the pieces come together in God's plan? We showed the film, shared the gospel of Christ, and lives were changed. Key connections for the church plant were made to that neighborhood through a unique use of Band-Aids and motorcycles.

"Whenever the Vargas film was shown, Satan worked to prevent it. At another church plant, a team experienced numerous problems when they tried to set up for showing the film. While workers tried to get all the equipment working, a man sat in his car nearby playing loud, banging music and clapping his hands. He would leave and return repeatedly with the same disruptive activity. But God's timing was perfect. When all the equipment was in place, the man became discouraged and left for good. Many people had time to gather and . . . be handed information about the church group. At the conclusion of that showing of the Vargas film, six people decided to follow Jesus.

"In all of my experiences with [outreach] teams, I have never been involved with such a mass number of people," Neil said. "I was amazed at the work accomplished at Extreme 2008 and the camaraderie that took place with so many different nationalities involved. It was truly God at work. I am always sad when it is time to leave a . . . site because the people have become such good friends. An experience like this causes a change in my heart and mind. I believe every Nazarene should go on an extended, overseas missions trip to see what Christians around the world have to deal with to accomplish the work of God."

EIGHT
TAKING CARE OF NEEDS

Dr. Tom Fitzpatrick participated in an Extreme 2008 medical team that included physician Dr. Paul McConnel and dentist Dr. Tom Dean. Argentine physician Dr. Martinez and his son Sebastian, who is a medical school student in Argentina, were also members of the team. Other medical personnel included a pharmacy technician, a nursing/dental hygienist, and a team of nurses.

"The medical team had two bases of operation," said Tom. "We traveled to El Bolson on our first trip and had a wonderful experience. We were able to meet with El Bolson officials as well as its medical community and members of the Mapuche tribe. We didn't provide as much medical intervention as we had anticipated. However, at the conclusion of our visit we realized we had helped raise awareness of the Church of the Nazarene in the area and opened doors for it to introduce Jesus to the residents of El Bolson and the local Mapuche tribe. Members of our medical team helped build a chapel for the Mapuche tribe, participated in showing the *JESUS* film in El Bolson, and enjoyed shopping at the local markets.

"From the medical aspect we did make house calls, and with the assistance of the local Nazarene church we provided medical and dental care for members of the Mapuche tribe. Most of the team members were able to join a local hospital medical team that provided clinics in the surrounding countryside. When we returned to Pilar, medical team members helped staff the compound infirmary."

Tom's 14-year-old daughter, Megan, accompanied him to Argentina. Here's her response to Extreme 2008. "During my time on the Argentina Extreme '08 [project], I was fortunate to go to El Bolson for one week with a medical team of 15 people. We visited several people's homes in the mountains. The Mapuche Indians have a tribal chief and their own customs, yet they are definitely Argentine. They manage to live and even thrive with few of the daily things we Americans view as necessities. I met a mountain family of a woman with two sons. They lived in a small hut and had to walk a half-mile to obtain drinking water in pop bottles. In comparison to them, we live privileged lives and take many things they only hear about for granted.

"Viewing and realizing these things gave me a greater understanding of diversity and helped me to grow as a person as I realized how easy I really have it. Plus, despite numerous hardships and a tough life, many members of the tribe had a great understanding and love for the Lord. I am extremely glad I got to experience another distinctive country and society."

"What impressed me most was the individual dedication of the leaders and people who came from all over the world to participate in Extreme 2008," said Tom. "Their efforts resulted in a successful outreach ministry that I believe will continue to bear fruit for many years. As a Catholic, what attracted me to that Extreme outreach effort was that sharing Jesus included the provision of food, clothing, and needed medical care as an integral part of evangelization. I am thankful for my opportunity to experience Extreme 2008. It's a time my daughter and I will not forget."

NINE
A CHANGE OF PLANS

From Brad the Dad:

"I wasn't expecting the Lord to whisper in my ear at the Karcher Church of the Nazarene Sunday morning service. But right in the middle of Brent Deakin's description of the KidsZone . . . opportunity in Argentina, I heard His voice: 'You need to change your travel plans, Brad. I don't want you and your family to fly to Hawaii in 2008 to celebrate your 20th wedding anniversary. Instead, I want you to take the funds you've been saving for two years and go to Argentina in 2007.' I had no doubts. God wanted my family to change its plans.

"That Sunday evening as we sat casually talking in the family room, I felt compelled to share the idea of a change of vacation plans with my wife, Tanya, and children, Robby and Katie, even though I feared they'd all immediately say, 'No way!' I took a deep breath and forced out the words. 'Mom and I haven't talked about this yet, but how would you feel if we went to Argentina in 2007 and not Hawaii in 2008?' I glanced at my wife, expecting an explosion any second. But instead of flat-out rejecting the idea, Tanya said, 'I need to tell you guys about my Sunday morning conversation with God.'"

From Tanya the Mom:

"As I sat listening to the speaker in church this morning, I heard God say, 'You don't need to go to Hawaii again.'

"I remember looking at the large cross in the church and questioning what I'd heard. 'Why would deciding to NOT go back to Hawaii be something good, God? We work hard, and we're saving money for the trip, while at the same time being faithful with our tithe.'

"With not even a pause, God repeated His message to me. 'You don't need to go to Hawaii again.' And then He added, 'You need to take your savings and start adding to it to pay for your family's trip to Argentina.'

"My heart turned strangely warm as I responded to God's words. 'OK, Lord. Now would You please tell Brad about this change of plans?'"

Looking at her husband, she continued. "I figured it would be weeks before you would say anything to us about Argentina. So just now, when you asked us how we would feel about going to Argentina, my jaw dropped. I knew at that very moment that God had answered my request . . . that we would change our plans . . . that all four of us would be going to Argentina."

Realizing that she had heard God literally speak to her in a voice that only she could hear—and that she would obey without question—was a wonderful moment for Tanya and her family.

From Robby the Son:

Like any 14-year-old boy, Robby was really looking forward to another vacation in Hawaii and the opportunity to visit family members who lived on the island of Oahu. "When my dad first talked to us about going to Argentina instead of Hawaii, I felt neither excited nor disappointed," he said. "It took me a few days to adjust to the change of plans. But as time went on, my excitement grew as I realized we were going to Argentina because that's where God wanted us to go."

From Katie the Daughter:

Eleven-year-old Katie also needed time to process the change. "When I first heard about KidsZone at church that Sunday morning, the thought crossed my mind that we might go," said Katie. "I was looking forward to learning how to surf in Hawaii. However, the more my family discussed Argentina, the more I knew God wanted me to go there, even though I had many fears about the trip."

PREPARATIONS

From Brad:

"It became clear that God was leading us to go to Argentina. The struggle would be in building up our savings so that we could swing a trip a year earlier than originally anticipated. But in His usual fashion, God supplied needed funds through gifts from family, friends, and even casual acquaintances. I was delighted at the thought of spending two weeks on the opposite side of the world, engaging with another culture, and experiencing God's hand moving in a mighty way."

From Tanya:

"The Lord provided for us financially in so many ways. Yet more importantly, He gave me peace. The fear that I normally would have felt when facing a trip to another country was slowly taken away as our departure date drew near. Because we four were going, my mother from Nampa and my cousin Shauna from Hawaii joined us for the journey."

JOB DESCRIPTIONS AT KIDSZONE 2007
From Brad:

"The Extreme Nazarene organizers assigned me to be in charge of the Extreme bank located in a small room on the seminary campus. Participants exchanged their U.S. dollars to pesos at the bank on a daily basis so they could buy souvenirs. Bank staff also paid vendors for supplies, equipment, and construction materials for the Bruno Radi Convention Center. All passports were held for safekeeping in the bank's safe.

"I was happy to help out in any way I could. But I honestly craved to do something other than what I normally did each day. I hoped to participate in a task that would utilize my studies of religion and experience in finance. About a week before we left for Argentina, I got a call from an Extreme organizer.

'We have a pastor who can't make the trip because of illness. Would you be willing to pastor one of the church plants?' Of course I said, 'Yes!'

"My church plant pastor responsibilities included leading the group that drove for three hours each way to the plant church in Villa Argentina on Saturdays and Sundays, organizing the small groups that distributed the evangelism materials in the neighborhood around the church, organizing the VBS program, and supporting the local Nazarene church pastor. I kept an attendance record of how many children and adults attended our events and of how many people accepted Christ as a result of our outreach programs. Getting the bank organized, figuring out what needed to be in place day-by-day for the church plant activities, and finding my daughter's lost luggage more than filled my days."

From Tanya:

"Originally, I was supposed to help Brad in the bank as a cash runner, but we both felt he had enough staff without me. Only three women were doing laundry for the 200 travelers, so my cousin Shauna and I asked them if they'd like some help. We'd leave for work most mornings before breakfast was over and return in the middle of dinner. Some days we did

50-plus loads of wash using five washers and dryers in four different locations. It took over two hours to dry a load, so the missionary wives would often fold a load or two for us in the evening or place a load in the dryer for us. Even though it wasn't the job I expected, it was wonderful to serve in this way.

"During our Saturdays in Villa Argentina our group worked on cleaning up the house and yards of a 75-year-old woman named Violeta. She lived close to our plant church. Her place was in horrible condition because the front yard, backyard, and house were full of garbage. Participants in Extreme 2008 later worked on the place as well. It was wonderful to view pictures of her functional home with the back and front yards showing off flower and food gardens."

From Robby:

"The teens did daily ministries together, like painting a church in one area and helping to build a small church in another area. I helped my aunt and mom and the other women with the laundry, helped in the kitchen, and [helped with] cleaning up the construction site. I played soccer with local kids, went to church, and helped clean up Violeta's house and yard. My favorite activity was passing [out] flyers

Robby and Katie at the work site

to teens at the local mall that invited them to attend a Christian rock . . . concert."

From Katie:

"I sanded doors and bars on the windows of the Bruno Radi Convention Center. I helped carry two-liter bottles of soda back to the kitchen to be set up for meals. Even though the bottles were heavy, I carried three bottles in my apron and a bottle in each hand. And I'm kind of small. After the meals, I carried dirty dishes to the kitchen for the dishwashing lady. I was involved with some of the daily teen ministries too."

REFLECTIONS

From Brad:

"My two weeks in Argentina seem like a whirlwind experience. As I walked through the neighborhood in Villa Argentina distributing flyers, I carried my digital camera. The local children were more than eager to pose for pictures and even more excited to see their faces on the camera's screen. I felt like a Pied Piper of sorts for many of them followed me throughout the neighborhood and back to the church for the children's program.

"Another experience that remains engrained in my mind is the conclusion of our last Sunday service in our Villa Argentina church plant. Pastor Claudio led our group and the local congregation in singing 'At the Cross.' We sang in English, and the locals [sang] in Spanish. I felt the Spirit of God fill the room as we lifted our voices in unison to praise His name. Tears flowed and hearts were unified in Christian love."

From Robby:

"[Memorable] moments include working on Violeta's house and property and learning that she became a Christian as a result of our cleaning up her place. Since I've been home, I feel grateful for what I have, and I'm much more concerned about people outside of the United States. I am going on a missions trip to Mexico in July."

From Katie:

"I thought it could maybe be fun to go to Argentina, only to find out it was fantastic! I found out how some people live and what kind of homes they live in. Now it's hard for me to be ungrateful. My most favorite part was doing the evangelism work near our church plant, Villa Argentina. I would do it all again. Now as I think about it, I realize my trip to Argentina changed me forever."

Katie and Violeta

From Tanya:

"My KidsZone experience is one I will treasure for the rest of my life. At our Villa Argentina church plant I met so many Argentines who loved the Lord and openly shared their faith. Violeta (the elderly woman whose property we cleaned up) came to one of our group's Sunday church services. At some point in our stay she had opened her heart to Jesus with the support of a Spanish-speaking pastor. We were able to talk with her, cry with her, and sing with her. It was like seeing a small glimpse of heaven. It's hard to put into words how it changed me to work at her home and to know that she has invited Jesus into her heart. My heart is overwhelmed with love when I think of her.

"Because of my participation in Extreme 2007, my heart has been opened wide to missions, and I will never be the same. My family hopes to be a part of the Extreme Amazon project in 2009. My prayer is that you who read our story will be open to hearing and obeying God's voice when He calls you to minister to others . . . whether in your hometown or in faraway places You'll be glad you did."

PRONUNCIATION GUIDE

Chapter 1
Garin — GAH-reen

Chapter 2
Jaguel — hah-GEHL

Chapter 3
Ezezia — eh-ZEH-zee-ah
Mariaelene Ruffinati — mah-ree-ah-eh-LAY-nay roo-fee-NAH-tee

Pozzi — POH-zee

Chapter 6
Ytreeide — yah-treh-IE-deh

Chapter 8
Mapuche — mah-POO-chee